Toys

PHASE 5

/oy/ie/

Level 5 – Green

Helpful Hints for Reading at Home

The graphemes (written letters) and phonemes (units of sound) used throughout this series are aligned with Letters and Sounds. This offers a consistent approach to learning whether reading at home or in the classroom.

HERE IS A LIST OF NEW PHONEMES FOR THIS PHASE OF LEARNING. AN EXAMPLE OF THE PRONUNCIATION CAN BE FOUND IN BRACKETS.

Phase 5			
ay (day)	ou (out)	ie (tie)	ea (eat)
oy (boy)	ir (girl)	ue (blue)	aw (saw)
wh (when)	ph (photo)	ew (new)	oe (toe)
au (Paul)	a_e (make)	e_e (these)	i_e (like)
o_e (home)	u_e (rule)		

Phase 5 Alternative Pronunciations of Graphemes			
a (hat, what)	e (bed, she)	i (fin, find)	o (hot, so, other)
u (but, unit)	c (cat, cent)	g (got, giant)	ow (cow, blow)
ie (tied, field)	ea (eat, bread)	er (farmer, herb)	ch (chin, school, chef)
y (yes, by, very)	ou (out, shoulder, could, you)		

HERE ARE SOME WORDS WHICH YOUR CHILD MAY FIND TRICKY.

Phase 5 Tricky Words			
oh	their	people	Mr
Mrs	looked	called	asked
could			

TOP TIPS FOR HELPING YOUR CHILD TO READ:

- Allow children time to break down unfamiliar words into units of sound and then encourage children to string these sounds together to create the word.

- Encourage your child to point out any focus phonics when they are used.

- Read through the book more than once to grow confidence.

- Ask simple questions about the text to assess understanding.

- Encourage children to use illustrations as prompts.

PHASE 5

/oy/ie/

This book focuses on the phonemes /oy/ and /ie/ and is a green level 5 book band.

How many words can you think of that have an **oy** sound?

Here are a few to get you started:

Boy

Toy

Toys are fun. There are lots of different toys to enjoy.

Toys to hug, toys that zoom and toys that go up and down. What can toys do?

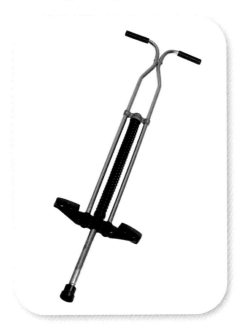

This toy flies up and down in the air. Have you got a toy that flies?

Now it is tied up! The boy and his dad need to untie the toy.

A doll can be held in a big hug. Dolls that are soft are good for hugging.

This boy enjoys sitting with his doll in the garden. Dolls are fun for all kids.

You can stack wooden blocks up. How high can you stack them?

It is hard to tap out the right block. When you tap it out, add it to the top.

Toy cars are fun to play with and fix.
Toy cars can be little or big.

Tap the cars along and get them to go zoom! Beep, beep. Honk the horn.

Some toys can go up and down. This toy is on a string. This one has a spring.

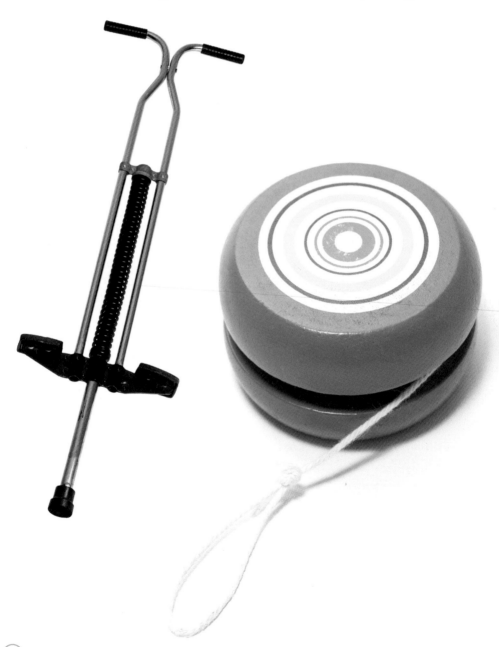

The spring in this toy is how it can go up and down. How long can you stay on?

©2022 **BookLife Publishing Ltd.**
King's Lynn, Norfolk PE30 4LS

ISBN 978-1-80155-104-5

All rights reserved. Printed in Poland.
A catalogue record for this book is available from
the British Library.

Toys
Written by Robin Twiddy
Designed by Gareth Liddington

An Introduction to BookLife Readers...

Our Readers have been specifically created in line with the London Institute of Education's approach to book banding and are phonetically decodable and ordered to support each phase of the Letters and Sounds document.

Each book has been created to provide the best possible reading and learning experience. Our aim is to share our love of books with children, providing both emerging readers and prolific page-turners with beautiful books that are guaranteed to provoke interest and learning, regardless of ability.

BOOK BAND GRADED using the Institute of Education's approach to levelling.

PHONETICALLY DECODABLE supporting each phase of Letters and Sounds.

EXERCISES AND QUESTIONS to offer reinforcement and to ascertain comprehension.

CLEAR DESIGN to inspire and provoke engagement, providing the reader with clear visual representations of each non-fiction topic.

AUTHOR INSIGHT:
ROBIN TWIDDY

Robin Twiddy is one of BookLife Publishing's most creative and prolific editorial talents, who imbues all his copy with a sense of adventure and energy. Robin's Cambridge-based first class honours degree in psychosocial studies offers a unique viewpoint on factual information and allows him to relay information in a manner that readers of any age are guaranteed to retain. He also holds a certificate in Teaching in the Lifelong Sector, and a post graduate certificate in Consumer Psychology.

A father of two, Robin has written over 70 titles for BookLife and specialises in conceptual, role-playing narratives which promote interaction with the reader and inspire even the most reluctant of readers to fully engage with his books.

PHASE 5

/oy/ie/

This book focuses on the phonemes /oy/ and /ie/ and is a green level 5 book band.

Image Credits Images are courtesy of Shutterstock.com. With thanks to Getty Images, Thinkstock Photo and iStockphoto. Cover – anitasstudio, Prostock-studio, Inara Prusakova, Veja, Gabberr. 3 – Pixel-Shot, Mauro Rodrigues, 4&5 – shoot4pleasure, Hurst Photo, Michael Kraus, KieferPix, natalia pak. 6&7 – Aleksei Potov, Butivshchenko Olena. 8&9 – MIA Studio, Oksana Kuzmina. 10&11 – fizkes, KAMONRAT 12&13 – Olesia Bilkei, Syda Productions. 14&15 – Lee Thompson Images, Elena Savva.